The Faculty
LOUNGE

The Faculty
LOUNGE

A Cocktail Guide
for Academics

Philipp STELZEL

INDIANA UNIVERSITY PRESS

This book is a publication of

INDIANA UNIVERSITY PRESS
Office of Scholarly Publishing
Herman B Wells Library 350
1320 East 10th Street
Bloomington, Indiana 47405 USA

iupress.org

Manufactured in the United States of America

First Printing 2023

Library of Congress Cataloging-in-Publication Data

Names: Stelzel, Philipp, author.
Title: The faculty lounge : a cocktail guide for academics / Philipp Stelzel.
Description: Bloomington, Indiana : Indiana University Press, 2023.
Identifiers: LCCN 2023016972 (print) | LCCN 2023016973 (ebook) |
ISBN 9780253067050 (hardback) | ISBN 9780253067067 (ebook)
Subjects: LCSH: Cocktails. | BISAC: COOKING / Beverages / Alcoholic / Bartending
& Cocktails | EDUCATION / Schools / Levels / Higher | LCGFT: Cookbooks.
Classification: LCC TX951 .S78 2023 (print) | LCC TX951
(ebook) | DDC 641.87/4—dc23/eng/20230417
LC record available at https://lccn.loc.gov/2023016972
LC ebook record available at https://lccn.loc.gov/2023016973

Contents

Acknowledgments

I'm particularly indebted to Sarah Bond and Josh Davis, who saw potential in my academic cocktails before I did, and to Benita Blessing for her crucial encouragement while I was working on this book. Benita and Margaret Menninger also invited me to host a cocktail hour at the German Studies Association conference in Indianapolis in October 2021, where participants gathered over the Forty-Minute Conference Paper and the 8 a.m. Panel.

My non-anonymous peer reviewers, Benita Blessing, Josh Davis, Sam Huneke, Jonathan Kaplan, Michael Mulvey, Molly Warsh, and especially Mark Boonshoft and Jay Shelat, deserve thanks for their comments and suggestions, which greatly benefited this book. I owe you all a few cocktails, including the Reader No. 2.

Terry Renaud, Bradley Proctor, Samuel Yates, Nolan Kline, Ben Hett, Astrid Eckert, Monica Black, Jennifer Evans, Jonathan Wiesen, Jay Geller, Anna Haensch, Danielle St. Hilaire, Becca Maatta, Matt Ussia, Daniel Selcer, John Mitcham, Aubrey Parke, Patrick Creisher, Lily Berry, Matt Gage, Jay Dietrichs, Karen Lautanen, Michelle Kienholz, Kate Snow, Sarah Greenwald, Nichole Mitcham, Klaus Sailer, Bretton Madden, Martin Mittermeier, Jacob Eder, Stefan Strasser, Steffi Riedl, and especially Michael Carroll provided good ideas and much-needed support along the way.

Starting a book project with one editor and finishing it with another can be challenging, but in this case, it worked out very well, as I benefited from the guidance and expertise of both Jennika Baines and Dan Crissman. At Indiana University Press, I also owe thanks to Darja Malcolm-Clarke for steering the book to completion and to Jennifer Witzke for the beautiful design.

Finally, a special thank-you to Moe, Monika, Wayne, Danny, and Mike—my very favorite Pittsburgh bartenders.

Introduction

ONE LATE AFTERNOON DURING THE EARLY WEEKS of the COVID-19 pandemic in March 2020, I felt like having a cocktail. The bars were closed, so I had to be my own bartender. I knew I wasn't in the mood for my usual favorite, a rye Manhattan. Instead, I mixed myself a drink whose ingredients were determined by what I happened to have at home that day—namely, bourbon, tart cranberry juice, and grenadine. The result struck me as acceptable for someone without formal bartending experience, and given the circumstances I named it the Social Distancer.

The following day, I saw someone on social media post a photo of a martini, referring to it as a "Quarantini."[1] Inspired, I made my own Quarantini, adding a splash of absinthe to a dry gin martini. Why? Because I drank it alone, while everybody else was *absinthe*.

---

1. Unfortunately, I have not been able to track down the original post, hence, no proper citation.

The Social Distancer

2 oz bourbon

1 oz tart cranberry juice

Splash of grenadine

Orange twist

Combine bourbon, tart cranberry juice, and grenadine in a mixing glass with ice. Stir and serve up with an orange twist.

Enjoy alone (which is what I did).

The Quarantini

2½ oz gin

½ oz dry white vermouth

Splash of absinthe

Lemon twist

Combine gin, dry white vermouth, and absinthe in a mixing glass with ice. Stir and serve up with a lemon twist.

Over the course of the following weeks, as I was struggling to adjust to remote teaching, I created a series of cocktail recipes around the theme of how academics were coping with the pandemic challenge. Soon, the Remote Instructor, the Self-Isolation Productivity Angst, the Canceled Conference, and the Cogito Ergo Zoom came into existence.

By the end of the semester, I had a library of about thirty drinks. I shared each recipe along with a photo of the cocktail on Twitter, and the responses to my tweets made me wonder whether I should include them in my annual self-evaluation under "service to the profession."

But while the challenges of teaching, researching, and writing in a pandemic were peculiar, other recipes—inspired by the regular conditions of academic life—also suggested themselves. After all, what professor would not thirst for a gin-based Presidential Platitude after enduring yet another town hall full of empty phrases and promises never to be fulfilled? Who would not reach for a rye-based Reply All Email after seeing yet another digital missive intended for the original sender but instead blasted to the hundreds of poor souls also on that mailing list? Who would turn down a rum-based Bored of Trustees after seeing that board make yet another poor choice regarding the university's leadership? And who would refuse a gin-based Question That Is More of a Comment after experiencing just that at a conference Q&A?

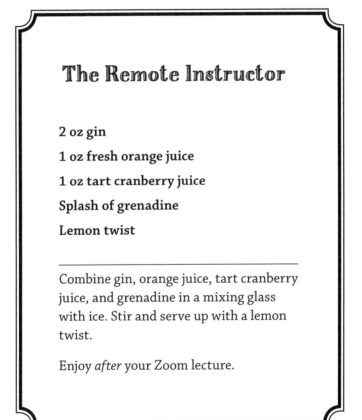

The Remote Instructor

2 oz gin

1 oz fresh orange juice

1 oz tart cranberry juice

Splash of grenadine

Lemon twist

Combine gin, orange juice, tart cranberry juice, and grenadine in a mixing glass with ice. Stir and serve up with a lemon twist.

Enjoy *after* your Zoom lecture.

The Self-Isolation Productivity Angst

2 oz bourbon

1 oz fresh orange juice

Splash of grenadine

1–2 dashes of orange bitters

Orange twist

Combine bourbon, orange juice, grenadine, and orange bitters in a mixing glass with ice. Stir and serve up with an orange twist.

Enjoy, and cut yourself some slack about not getting any writing done.

Clearly, there are many aspects of academic life that call for a cocktail. A mixed drink can help with coping and commiseration. Perhaps most importantly, a cocktail facilitates new connections, whether at a conference hotel bar or, more recently, over Zoom. I have been fortunate to experience the communal aspect of our profession early on; "academic community," therefore, is not an empty phrase to me. And I believe that in light of the current, severe challenges higher education is facing almost everywhere, fostering the community of academics has never been more essential. To keep that community lubricated, this book offers suggestions, along with consolation, and (I hope) amusement.

The cocktail recipes that follow are grouped according to the six areas of academic life when they are best enjoyed. The final chapter is for toasting intellectuals in your field.

Most of the recipes call for ingredients that are easy to obtain. This book will not unnecessarily complicate the notion of a good libation but will instead challenge the hegemony of libational complexity. Thus, you generally will not have to interrogate the liminal spaces of your kitchen cabinet for celery bitters. Neither will you have to rethink whether or not that rhubarb syrup you once concocted is still good to use. Nonetheless, you may want to problematize which kind of liquor you prefer (and to consult the list of cocktails by liquor and cordial at the end to find your favorites). Then it's time to purchase, unpack, and utilize the ingredients, and to contextualize the cocktail in its proper glass.

The Canceled Conference

2 oz gin

1 oz pomegranate juice

1 oz fresh lemon juice

Splash of simple syrup

1–2 dashes of cherry bitters

Lemon twist

Combine gin, pomegranate juice, lemon juice, simple syrup, and cherry bitters in a mixing glass with ice. Stir and serve up with a lemon twist.

Enjoy after you've finally gotten hold of an airline representative to refund your flight.

The Cogito Ergo Zoom

2 oz bourbon

1 oz tart cherry juice

Splash of simple syrup (optional)

1–2 dashes of cherry bitters

Lemon twist

Combine bourbon, tart cherry juice, simple syrup (if desired), and cherry bitters in a mixing glass with ice. Stir and serve up with a lemon twist.

Enjoy with your camera turned off.

With a few exceptions (noted), I recommend serving the following cocktails up and the mocktails on ice. But this is a cocktail book for academics; thus, my recipes are open to interpretation and reconsideration. And Reader No. 2 will likely tell you that I got it wrong anyway.

Cheers!

FOR THE GRADUATE STUDENT

WHEN I WAS A STUDENT AT A STATE university with meager graduate stipends, my budget did not allow me to assemble a cocktail bar at home, but the following are the drinks I would have mixed for myself if it had. Except for the Library Fine (which I somehow managed to avoid), they are based on my own experiences.

The Teaching Assistant

2 oz dark rum

½ oz fresh orange juice

Coke to taste

Lime wedge

Fill a tumbler with ice, then add rum and orange juice. Stir, and then add Coke. Serve with a lime wedge.

A quick and easy drink, so you can get back to grading or class prep.

The recipe was provided by the professor, who most likely has been listing the same ingredients for the last twenty years.

The Dissertation Committee

2 oz dark rum

1 oz tart cherry juice

1 oz fresh orange juice

1 oz fresh lemon juice

Splash of simple syrup

1–2 dashes of orange bitters

Orange twist

Combine rum, tart cherry juice, orange juice, lemon juice, simple syrup, and orange bitters in a mixing glass with ice. Stir and serve up with an orange twist.

Apart from rum, this cocktail contains five ingredients, but you'll only ever be able to get ahold of four of them at the same time.

The Comprehensive Exams

2 oz bourbon

1 oz pomegranate juice

1 oz lemon juice

Splash of simple syrup

Lemon twist

Combine bourbon, pomegranate juice, lemon juice, and simple syrup in a mixing glass with ice. Stir and serve up with a lemon twist.

For this cocktail, you're required to purchase several dozen different kinds of liquor and nonalcoholic ingredients, but only four will ultimately become part of the drink.

The Library Fine

1 oz tart cherry juice

1 oz fresh orange juice

Club soda to taste

Lemon wedge

Fill a tumbler with ice, then add tart cherry and orange juice. Stir. Add club soda. Serve with a lemon wedge.

A tart mocktail, since paying that fine has cut into your liquor budget.

The Classmate Who Hasn't Read but Talks Anyway

2–3 oz vodka

1 oz fresh orange juice

Splash of Green Chartreuse

2–3 dashes of orange bitters (optional, depending on how annoying that classmate's comments are)

Orange wedge

Fill a tumbler with ice. Add vodka, orange juice, Green Chartreuse, and the bitters (if using). Stir and serve with an orange wedge.

Enjoy preferably during (or else after) class.

FOR THE FACULTY MEMBER

ARE YOU ABOUT TO ASSUME A departmental service role?

Are you facing the prospect of another three-hour faculty meeting?

Are you a junior faculty member who was just "kindly asked" to sit on that brand-new University Committee for Learning Outcome Metrics Redesign Preparation?

Are you a department chair currently working on next semester's teaching schedule?

These recipes are for you.

The Professor's Punch

2 oz dark rum

1 oz lime juice

1 oz fresh orange juice

1 oz tart cherry juice

Splash of grenadine

1–2 dashes of cherry bitters

Maraschino cherry or pineapple wedge

Combine rum, lime juice, orange juice, tart cherry juice, grenadine, and orange bitters in a mixing glass with ice. Stir, strain into a tumbler over ice, and serve with a maraschino cherry or a pineapple wedge.

A classic for the professor who is dreaming of a tropical island vacation (or a visit to the archives at least) but instead is facing office hours and a faculty meeting.

The Faculty Meeting

2 oz rye

1 oz pomegranate juice

1–2 dashes of orange bitters

Orange twist

Combine rye, pomegranate juice, and orange bitters in a mixing glass with ice. Stir and serve up with an orange twist.

Have (at least) one prior to the meeting.

The Desolate Department Chair

2 oz vodka

1 oz tart cherry juice

½ oz fresh lemon juice

Splash of simple syrup

1–2 dashes of cherry bitters

Lemon twist

Combine vodka, tart cherry juice, lemon juice, simple syrup, and cherry bitters in a mixing glass with ice. Stir and serve up with a lemon twist.

Enjoy, and get to work on the twenty-seventh iteration of next semester's teaching schedule before you send out the long agenda for the next faculty meeting.

The Annual Self-Evaluation

2 oz rye

1 oz tart cherry juice

1 oz fresh orange juice

Splash of absinthe

Splash of simple syrup

Orange twist

Combine rye, tart cherry juice, orange juice, absinthe, and simple syrup in a mixing glass with ice. Stir and serve up with an orange twist.

Enjoy after you have mastered the brand-new online portal your university has acquired for submitting such evaluations.

The Academic Politics

2 oz scotch

2 oz fresh orange juice

Splash of simple syrup

Several dashes of orange bitters, for obvious reasons

Maraschino cherry

Combine scotch, orange juice, simple syrup, and orange bitters in a mixing glass with ice. Stir and serve up with a maraschino cherry.

"Academic politics are so nasty because the stakes are so low" is a quote attributed (in similar forms) to several individuals, including president of the University of Chicago Robert M. Hutchins (1899–1977), philosopher and founding director of the National Humanities Center Charles Frankel (1917–1979), and political scientist Wallace S. Sayre (1905–1972).

Enjoy this tasty cocktail while getting ready for the next petty conflict.

The Reply All Email

2 oz rye

1 oz fresh orange juice

Splash of grenadine

1–2 dashes of orange bitters

Orange twist

Combine rye, orange juice, grenadine, and orange bitters in a mixing glass with ice. Stir and serve up with an orange twist.

Take a deep breath as you read yet another email replying to the original sender "Congrats, Jack!" or demanding in all caps "PLEASE TAKE ME OFF THIS LIST IMMEDIATELY," and enjoy.

The Repeated Reply All Email

3 oz rye

Slowly pour the rye into a mason jar.

Down in one gulp, between tears.

Repeat.

The Furloughed Football Coach

2 oz vodka

1 oz concord grape juice

1 oz fresh lemon juice

Splash of simple syrup

Lemon wedge

Combine vodka, concord grape juice, lemon juice, and simple syrup in a mixing glass with ice. Stir and serve up with a lemon wedge.

Of course, this cocktail does not actually exist. After all, the coach is an "essential worker" whose employment is central to the university's mission.

The Two-Faced Town Hall

2 oz white rum

1 oz fresh orange juice

1 oz tart cherry juice

Splash of simple syrup

1–2 dashes of orange bitters

Orange twist

Combine rum, orange juice, tart cherry juice, simple syrup, and orange bitters in a mixing glass with ice. Stir and serve up with an orange twist.

Enjoy, and know how much we appreciate your dedication to the mission of our university, until your contract expires.

The University Mission Statement

2 oz vodka

1 oz pomegranate juice

1 oz fresh lemon juice

Splash of grenadine

1–2 dashes of orange bitters

Orange twist

Combine vodka, pomegranate juice, lemon juice, grenadine, and orange bitters in a mixing glass with ice. Stir and serve up with an orange twist.

Ponder how tasty this cocktail would be. Then remember the reality on campus, pour out the cocktail, and have a shot of vinegar instead.

The Forgotten Faculty Senate

2 oz gin

1 oz dry white vermouth

1 oz concord grape juice

1 oz fresh lime juice

Splash of simple syrup

Lemon twist

Combine gin, dry white vermouth, concord grape juice, lime juice, and simple syrup in a mixing glass with ice. Stir and serve up with a lemon twist.

Enjoy, and dream of shared governance.

The Wellness Webinar

2 oz ginger beer

2 oz tart cherry juice

Club soda to taste

Lemon wedge

Fill a tumbler with ice, then add ginger beer, tart cherry juice, and club soda. Stir briefly. Serve with a lemon wedge.

Register for the webinar. On second thought, pour yourself two ounces of bourbon instead.

The University
Rebranding Strategy

Lots of moving parts:

Nimbly reach out to vodka (2 oz)

Pivot to tart cranberry juice (2 oz)

Circle back to fresh lime juice (1 oz)

Then leverage Green Chartreuse (a splash)

Follow up with a lime wedge

Robust deliverable: a good cocktail.

Combine vodka, tart cranberry juice, lime juice, and Green Chartreuse in a mixing glass with ice. Stir and serve up with a lime wedge.

I recommend having at least two of these cocktails after enduring a meeting filled with business jargon.

The Brand-New Athletics Complex

2 oz concord grape juice

1 oz fresh lime juice

Splash of simple syrup

Club soda to taste

Lime wedge

Fill a tumbler with ice, then add concord grape juice, lime juice, and simple syrup. Stir, and then add club soda. Serve with a lime wedge.

This is obviously a mocktail, since the money that would have been spent on liquor was reallocated to support the new athletics facility.

We trust you'll understand.

The Committee
Assessment Committee

2 ½ oz fresh orange juice

2 ½ oz club soda

Pour the orange juice into a flute glass, then gently add the club soda and stir.

Enjoy as long as your committee work lasts, which means that this will be the nonalcoholic equivalent of a bottomless mimosa.

FOR
TEACHING
AND
GRADING

A RE YOU TEACHING A HIGHER COURSE LOAD this semester?

Are you about to grade several dozen exams?

Are you trying to decide how to handle a suspected case of plagiarism?

Are you about to read your course evaluations?

Did you just receive an email from a student who did not attend class and is now asking you if they "missed anything important"?

This chapter covers the accompanying drinks.

The Increased Teaching Load

2 oz tequila blanco

1 oz tart cranberry juice

1 oz fresh lemon juice

Splash of grenadine

Lemon twist

Combine tequila, tart cranberry juice, lemon juice, and grenadine in a mixing glass with ice. Stir and serve up with a lemon twist.

Enjoy with a heavy dose of gallows humor.

The Unread Syllabus

2 oz tequila blanco

1 oz pomegranate juice

1 oz fresh lime juice

Splash of simple syrup

Lime wedge

Combine tequila, pomegranate juice, lime juice, and simple syrup in a mixing glass with ice. Stir and serve up with a lime wedge.

As someone whose syllabi, despite multiple rounds of proofreading, routinely contain errors, I am of two minds on the issue of students not paying close attention to the syllabus. After all, this gives me a chance to correct those errors before they notice.

The Dear Ms. Smith

2 oz rye

2 oz fresh orange juice

1 oz fresh lime juice

Splash of grenadine

Orange twist

Combine rye, orange juice, lime juice, and grenadine in a mixing glass with ice. Stir and serve up with an orange twist.

A cocktail for Dr. Smith, after she receives yet another email from a student omitting her title.

The Extra Credit Assignment

No ingredients given, as this drink should not exist on the college level.

The Sorry I Wasn't in Class Today, Did I Miss Anything Important?

2 oz scotch, neat

Take a sip and a deep breath and suppress the urge to reply with snark. Or perhaps don't.

The Course Evaluation

2 oz scotch

1 oz tart cranberry juice

1 oz fresh lime juice

Splash of simple syrup

Lime wedge

Combine scotch, tart cranberry juice, lime juice, and simple syrup in a mixing glass with ice. Stir and serve up with a lime wedge.

A cocktail free from the myriad of biases that render end-of-semester course evaluations fairly worthless.

The I Really Enjoyed
Your Class

2 oz vodka

1 oz fresh orange juice

1 oz fresh lemon juice

Splash of grenadine

Lemon twist

Combine vodka, orange juice, lemon juice, and grenadine in a mixing glass with ice. Stir and serve up with a lemon twist.

Traditionally a seasonal cocktail, especially popular at the end of the semester.

The Stack of Exams

2 oz scotch

1 oz tart cherry juice

1 oz fresh lemon juice

Splash of simple syrup

1–2 dashes of cherry bitters

Lemon twist

Combine scotch, tart cherry juice, lemon juice, simple syrup, and cherry bitters in a mixing glass with ice. Stir and serve up with a lemon twist.

Depending on the exams' quality, a refill may be necessary.

The Plagiarist

2 oz rye

¾–1 oz red vermouth

1–2 dashes of cherry bitters

Maraschino cherry

Combine rye, red vermouth, and cherry bitters in a mixing glass with ice. Stir and serve up with a maraschino cherry.

The student has replaced Angostura bitters with cherry bitters, confident that the professor won't notice that this is still a Manhattan recipe.

FOR THE CONFERENCE ATTENDEE

MANY OF US ASSOCIATE ACADEMIC conferences with overpriced glasses of wine and cans of beer at hotel bars. This chapter suggests some alternatives, and mixing these cocktails at home will be less expensive than ordering a glass of wine between the last panel and dinner.

The Forty-Minute Conference Paper

2½ oz rye

1 oz Cointreau (or other triple sec liqueur)

1 oz fresh lemon juice

Lemon twist

Combine rye, Cointreau, and lemon juice in a mixing glass with ice. Stir and serve up with a lemon twist.

Take a long sip anytime the presenter assures the audience that they are "coming to the end."

The Question That Is More of a Comment

2 oz gin

2 oz concord grape juice

1 oz fresh lemon juice

Splash of simple syrup

Lemon twist

Combine gin, concord grape juice, lemon juice, and simple syrup in a mixing glass with ice. Stir and serve up with a lemon twist.

Enjoy, and respond with a smile.

The I Don't Mean to Interrupt Your Conversation . . .

2 oz bourbon

2 oz fresh orange juice

1 oz tart cherry juice

Splash of grenadine

Orange twist

Combine bourbon, orange juice, tart cherry juice, and grenadine in a mixing glass with ice. Stir and serve up with an orange twist.

This cocktail is best enjoyed during conference receptions and in hotel lobbies.

The 8 a.m. Panel

3 oz fresh orange juice

2 oz tart cranberry juice

1 oz fresh lemon juice

Splash of grenadine

Lemon wedge

Fill a tumbler with ice. Add orange juice, tart cranberry juice, lemon juice, and grenadine. Stir and serve with a lemon wedge.

Optional: Enjoy with one or two aspirin, depending on how many times you ordered the Question That Is More of a Comment the previous evening.

The Hotel Bar Experience

1 can of PBR

_____

Open the can.
Burn a ten-dollar bill.
Repeat.

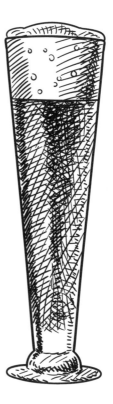

The Travel Expenses Reimbursement

2 oz bourbon

1 oz pomegranate juice

1 oz fresh lime juice

Splash of grenadine

Lemon twist

Combine bourbon, pomegranate juice, lime juice, and grenadine in a mixing glass with ice. Stir and serve up with a lemon twist.

Before adding each ingredient, fill out a form explaining, in no more than one hundred words, why the ingredient is necessary. Submit the form, then wait at least three months before enjoying the drink.

The Sunday Morning Slot

2 oz vodka

1½ oz espresso

Splash of simple syrup

Dash of orange bitters

Orange twist

Combine vodka, espresso, simple syrup, and orange bitters in a mixing glass with ice. Stir and serve up with an orange twist.

You might as well enjoy this cocktail before your panel, as the small and likely sleepy audience will mean you can get away with being intoxicated.

The Flight-Delayed Scholar

2 oz gin

1 oz fresh orange juice

1 oz fresh lemon juice

Splash of simple syrup

Several dashes of orange bitters

Lemon twist

Combine gin, orange juice, lemon juice, simple syrup, and orange bitters in a mixing glass with ice. Stir and serve up with a lemon twist.

A drink slightly less tart than this travel experience.

FOR
RESEARCHING
AND
WRITING

U NLIKE FICTION—THINK ERNEST
Hemingway, Dorothy Parker, or Richard
Yates, for example—academic writing is
less often associated with drinking (except
unhealthy quantities of coffee). Yet, as this
chapter suggests, there are numerous writing-
and research-related occasions that call for
a cocktail, whether it's the good news of
receiving a research fellowship or a much-
dreaded reader report.

The Research Fellowship

2 oz scotch

1 oz tart cherry juice

1 oz fresh orange juice

1–2 dashes of orange bitters

Maraschino cherry

Combine scotch, tart cherry juice, orange juice, and orange bitters in a mixing glass with ice. Stir and serve up with a maraschino cherry.

Enjoy after a day of writing and not checking your university email.

The Sabbatical

½ oz Cointreau

½ oz fresh lemon juice

Champagne to taste

Combine Cointreau and lemon juice in a mixing glass with ice. Stir, strain, and then add champagne.

You may enjoy this cocktail once every seven years, unless you get somebody else to buy the champagne.

The Inaccessible Archive

2 oz gin

½ oz Green Chartreuse

1 oz fresh orange juice

Orange twist

Combine gin, Green Chartreuse, and orange juice in a mixing glass with ice. Stir and serve up with an orange twist.

Yes, Chartreuse is a bit pricey, but you will be saving a lot of money by not going to the archives.

The First Draft

2 oz of liquor

1–2 oz of juice

Perhaps one or two ounces of another juice?

Bitters? I'm not quite sure yet.

Up or on ice?

TBD tomorrow.

After all, I have grading to do.

The Reader No. 2

The author has proposed to make this a gin-based (2 oz) cocktail.

Yet as I have argued elsewhere (work with which the author has failed to engage), in this context, bourbon is the methodologically superior choice. Please provide the correct citation as well.

The author's argument for tart cranberry juice (2 oz) lacks sufficient empirical evidence; concord grape juice (2 oz) is the logical alternative.

The proposition of adding fresh lemon juice (1 oz) has been debunked by recent literature on the subject; hence, the author should consider fresh lime juice (1 oz).

While I appreciate the idea of adding grenadine to the existing scholarship, simple syrup is a theoretically more sophisticated choice.

To reach a broader audience, serve on ice, not up.

Once the cocktail has been modified accordingly, I would be willing to try it again.

The Revise and Resubmit

Consider mixing the Reader No. 2.

Instead make yourself two cups of strong coffee.

Add a sugar cube or two, along with a dash of orange bitters.

Stir, and get to work.

The Principal Investigator

2 oz tequila blanco

1 oz Aperol

1 oz Green Chartreuse

1 oz fresh lime juice

Lime wedge

Combine tequila, Aperol, Green Chartreuse, and lime juice in a mixing glass with ice. Stir and serve up with a lime wedge.

This recipe has been drafted by the PI, yet the cocktail was mixed by a postdoc and a grad student.

The Twelve-Hour Time Point

2 oz vodka

1 oz fresh orange juice

1 oz fresh lemon juice

½ oz Green Chartreuse

Splash of simple syrup

Orange twist

Combine vodka, orange juice, lemon juice, Green Chartreuse, and simple syrup in a mixing glass with ice. Stir and serve up with an orange twist.

Enjoy, and then get some sleep (at home, not in the lab).

The Writer's Block

. . . .

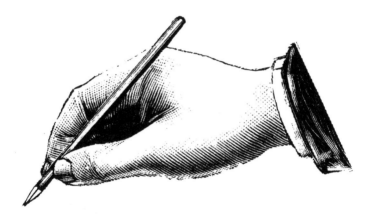

The Page Proofs

2 oz tart cranberry juice

2 oz fresh orange juice

1 oz fresh lime juice

Splash of grenadine

Club soda to taste

Fill a tumbler with ice and add tart cranberry juice, orange juice, lime juice, and grenadine. Stir and then add club soda.

This tart mocktail will help you keep a sharp focus while looking for typos.

FOR THE
ADMINISTRATOR

THERE ARE PROBABLY FEW THINGS THAT
make academics long for a strong
drink more than having to face university
administrators. Whether it is a presidential
speech largely detached from the reality
on campus, a provost's town hall certain
to raise one's blood pressure, or an email
to all faculty announcing the creation of
yet another senior vice president position
whose utility appears questionable, there
are plenty of reasons to have a tasty cocktail
to soothe your righteous indignation.

The Ass. Dean's Dream

Faculty: 3 oz tap water

Associate deans and deans: replace tap water with 2 oz gin

Associate/vice provosts and provost: replace gin with 4–5 oz champagne

1 oz tart cranberry juice

½ oz fresh lemon juice

Splash of simple syrup

1–2 dashes of orange bitters

Lemon twist

Combine whichever first ingredient your status allows you (i.e., tap water or gin—but not champagne), tart cranberry juice, lemon juice, simple syrup, and orange bitters in a mixing glass with ice.

Stir (for provost's version, strain, then add champagne) and serve up with a lemon twist.

The Presidential Platitude

2 oz gin

1 oz fresh orange juice

1 oz pomegranate juice

Splash of grenadine

Several dashes of orange bitters

Orange twist

Combine gin, orange juice, pomegranate juice, grenadine, and orange bitters in a mixing glass with ice. Stir and serve up with an orange twist.

Enjoy, and please know how much I appreciate your willingness to go that extra mile on behalf of our university family during these trying times.

The Pontificating Provost

2 oz white rum

1 oz tart cherry juice

1 oz fresh lemon juice

Splash of simple syrup

1–2 dashes of cherry bitters

Lemon twist

Combine white rum, tart cherry juice, lemon juice, simple syrup, and cherry bitters in a mixing glass with ice. Stir and serve up with a lemon twist.

Enjoy, dear faculty colleagues, as you approach the new semester with intentionality.

The Clueless CFO

2 oz bourbon

Club soda to taste

Fill a tumbler with ice, then rightsize the amount of bourbon from two ounces to one ounce.

Move the needle by adding club soda to taste.

Table the conversation on adding anything else, because of budget constraints.

Enjoy, and prepare yourself to counter bad-faith arguments and flawed financial data compiled to undermine your department or program.

The Senior Vice President for Unspecified Administrative Excellence

1 oz vodka

1 oz Cointreau

4–5 oz champagne

Combine vodka and Cointreau in a mixing glass with ice. Stir. Strain into a coupe glass, and then top off with champagne.

Enjoy as you contemplate how many perfectly decent cocktails you could have bought for the price of the champagne.

The Bored of Trustees

2 oz white rum

1 oz tart cranberry juice

1 oz fresh lime juice

Splash of grenadine

Lime wedge

Combine white rum, tart cranberry juice, lime juice, and grenadine in a mixing glass with ice. Stir and serve up with a lime wedge.

Enjoy while you're explaining the value of your discipline to businesspeople and lawyers.

The Tequila (Program) Sunset

2 oz tequila blanco

2 oz fresh orange juice

1 oz fresh lemon juice

1 oz tart cherry juice

Splash of grenadine

Lemon twist

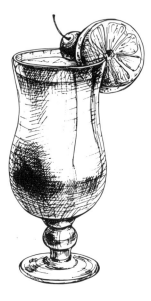

Combine tequila, orange juice, lemon juice, tart cherry juice, and grenadine in a mixing glass with ice. Stir very carefully; you might wake up an administrator. Then serve up with a lemon twist.

TOAST
YOUR
FAVORITE
INTELLECTUAL

A FEW YEARS AGO, I READ IN A BIOGRAPHY of the renowned American historian Richard Hofstadter about his habit of serving graduate students a gin and tonic when grilling them on their comprehensive exam questions. This gave me the idea of creating cocktails related to important intellectual figures. The following recipes were inspired by the scholars' work rather than their drink preferences.

The Fernand Braudel

2 oz cognac

2 oz fresh orange juice

1 oz fresh lemon juice

Splash of simple syrup

1–2 dashes of orange bitters

Rosemary sprig

Combine cognac, orange juice, lemon juice, simple syrup, and orange bitters in a mixing glass with ice. Stir and serve up, garnished with rosemary.

As a structure of one's everyday life, this cocktail might cause a longue durée of intoxication.

FERNAND BRAUDEL (1902–1985) was a French historian and important member of the Annales School whose works include a multivolume history of the Mediterranean.

The Max Weber

1–2 oz concord grape juice + 3 oz club soda (Protestant ethic)

2 oz gin (spirit of capitalism)

Fill a tumbler with ice. Add gin and concord grape juice. Stir. Add club soda.

Enjoy when you can afford it.

Please note: this recipe is only an ideal type in the Weberian sense.

MAX WEBER (1864–1920) was a German sociologist and political economist widely considered to be one of the main architects of modern social science.

The Werner Heisenberg

The recipe's principle is uncertain.

WERNER HEISENBERG (1901–1976) was a German
theoretical physicist and one of the pioneers of
quantum mechanics.

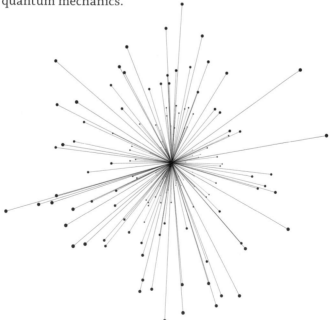

The Gin-der as Performance
(a Judith Butler Cocktail)

2 oz gin

2 oz tart cherry juice

1 oz dry white vermouth

1–2 dashes of cherry bitters

Lemon twist

Combine gin, tart cherry juice, dry white vermouth, and cherry bitters in a mixing glass with ice.

Stir and serve up with a lemon twist.

JUDITH BUTLER (b. 1956) is an American philosopher and social theorist whose work has been influential within political philosophy, ethics, literary theory, and queer theory.

The Ste. Sophie Germain

2 oz St. Germain liqueur

Splash of fresh lemon juice

2^2+1 oz club soda

Fresh mint

Fill a tumbler with ice. Add St. Germain liqueur and lemon juice. Stir and add club soda. Serve with mint as garnish.

This is a rather light cocktail, so you can still work on number theory.

SOPHIE (MARIE-SOPHIE) GERMAIN (1776–1831) was a French mathematician known for her contributions to number theory.

Paul Erdős's Poison

2 oz pálinka (Hungarian fruit brandy) or comparable apricot or plum brandy

5–6 oz strong coffee

Splash of simple syrup or dash of sugar

In a mug, combine brandy, coffee, and simple syrup. Stir.

Enjoy as you search for coauthors who will lower your Erdős number.

PAUL ERDŐS (1913–1996) was a Hungarian mathematician known for his prolific research output (he published almost 1,500 papers) and his many (over 500) collaborations. The Erdős number describes the "collaborative distance" between the mathematician and another person, measured by authorship of mathematical papers. Erdős consumed large quantities of coffee as well as amphetamines but considered alcohol to be "poison."

The Marie Curie

2 oz vodka (preferably Polish, e.g., Belvedere, Luksosowa, or Sobieski)

1 oz Green Chartreuse

Fresh mint

Combine vodka and Green Chartreuse in a mixing glass with ice.

Stir and serve up with fresh mint as garnish.

MARIE CURIE (1867–1934) was a Polish and later naturalized French physicist and chemist known for her pioneering research on radioactivity. She was a two-time Nobel Prize winner.

The Margaret Mead

2 oz dark rum

1 oz fresh orange juice

1 oz fresh lime juice

Honey (it's Mead, after all . . .) to taste

1–2 dashes of orange bitters

Orange twist

Combine dark rum, orange juice, lime juice, honey, and orange bitters in a mixing glass with ice.

Stir and serve up with an orange twist.

MARGARET MEAD (1901–1978) was an American cultural anthropologist known for her study *Coming of Age in Samoa* and her public-facing engagement.

The W. E. B. Du Bois

2 oz bourbon

1 oz Cointreau

1 oz fresh orange juice

1 oz fresh lemon juice

Orange twist

Combine bourbon, Cointreau, orange juice, and lemon juice in a mixing glass with ice. Stir and serve up with an orange twist.

An interdisciplinary cocktail, not only for historians and sociologists. The liqueur is French; the drink's pronunciation is not.

W. E. B. DU BOIS (1868–1963) was an American historian, sociologist, and civil rights activist and one of the founders of the National Association for the Advancement of Colored People (NAACP).

Epilogue

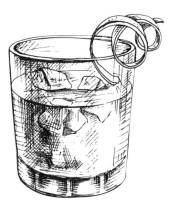

The Very Last Word

1 oz gin

½ oz mezcal

1½ oz Campari

1½ oz red vermouth

Orange twist

Combine gin, mezcal, Campari, red vermouth, and orange bitters in a mixing glass with ice.

Stir and strain over ice with an orange twist.

Apart from gin, this cocktail has nothing in common with the Prohibition-era Last Word, which also contains lime juice, Green Chartreuse, and maraschino liqueur.

But a drink with this name seemed like an appropriate way to conclude a cocktail book for academics, and this Very Last Word contains four ingredients with strong and distinguishable flavors.

A Note on Ingredients

P ARTICULARLY FOR THE TART, fruit juice–heavy cocktails, I consider top-shelf liquor unnecessary.

For gin-based cocktails, I recommend any London Dry gin. Those with a distinct juniper note (such as Tanqueray) will hold themselves better against other ingredients with stronger flavors.

BOURBON I have been using Maker's Mark, Old Forester, and Old Grand Dad.

RYE I have been using Dickel and Old Overholt Bonded.

SCOTCH I have been using Grant's Blended Scotch.

VODKA I have been using Svedka.

TEQUILA I have been using Sauza Silver.

RUM I have been using a local white and dark rum (Maggie's Farm, Pittsburgh). Bacardi (white) and Appleton Estate Signature Blend (dark) are far easier to obtain.

MEZCAL I have been using Monte Alban.

VERMOUTH Cocktail snobs will be upset, but I have been using Martini & Rossi red vermouth. Noilly Prat is my dry white vermouth of choice (here, too, Reader No. 2 might disagree).

CRANBERRY JUICE Do not use "cranberry juice cocktail," which only contains just over a quarter of actual cranberry juice, mixed with other juices and added sugar. Instead, use tart cranberry juice, which does not contain any additions (or at least no additional sweeteners).

GRAPE JUICE I have been using pure concord grape juice.

CHERRY JUICE I have been using pure tart cherry juice.

CITRUS JUICES I recommend squeezing fresh oranges rather than using orange juice made from concentrate. Since bottled lemon and lime juice (not made from concentrate) are usually easier to find and closer to the freshly squeezed variant, I have used those instead of squeezing fresh lemons or limes.

BITTERS I have been using Angostura bitters, Angostura orange bitters, and Fee Brothers cherry bitters.

Tools

GLASSWARE

For cocktails served up, go with a *coupe glass*—even more elegant than the prose in your annual self-evaluation. Alternatively, use a *martini glass*, which is most likely the choice of Reader No. 2.

For cocktails served on ice, use a *rocks glass* (sometimes also called a *short tumbler*), a glass as solid as your reasons for declining to serve on yet another university committee.

EQUIPMENT

Rather than using a shaker, go with a *mixing glass*, as all the cocktails in this book should be stirred rather than shaken. That way your drink will remain as clear and transparent as your university's administrative decisions.

A *jigger* (1 oz and ½ oz) will help you measure your drink's ingredients, and it will also fit the "raise" you may or may not be getting this year.

Very important is a *bar spoon* or *stirring spoon*. It should be long and thin, just like your university president's commencement speech.

You will also need a *strainer* (preferably a *Hawthorne strainer*), so you can strain your cocktail just as thoroughly as the next faculty meeting will certainly strain your nerves.

Finally, you will need a *channel knife* (or, alternatively, a *vegetable peeler*) to create your lemon and orange twists, as thin as your senior administrators' skin when you challenge their newest "cost containment" plans at a town hall.

Cocktails by Liquor and Cordial

MOCKTAILS

RUM (DARK)

RUM (WHITE)

RYE

VODKA

FOR INDIANA UNIVERSITY PRESS

Emily Baugh *Editorial Assistant*

Tony Brewer *Artist and Book Designer*

Brian Carroll *Rights Manager*

Dan Crissman *Trade and Regional Acquisitions Editor*

Samantha Heffner *Trade Acquisitions Assistant*

Brenna Hosman *Production Coordinator*

Katie Huggins *Production Manager*

Darja Malcolm-Clarke *Project Manager and Editor*

Dan Pyle Online *Publishing Manager*

Rachel Rosolina *Marketing Manager*

Jennifer L. Witzke *Senior Artist and Book Designer*